FROM BROKE TO BUST STEP BY STEP GUIDE TO SURVIVE AS COPYWRITER

Soham M.

Copyright © 2016

All rights reserved. No part of this book may be reproduced or transmitted in any form or by any means, electronic or mechanical, including photocopying, recording or by any information storage and retrieval system without written permission of the publisher, except for the inclusion of brief quotations in a review.

INTRODUCTION	4
CHAPTER ONE	6
CHAPTER TWO	19
CHAPTER THREE	28
CHAPTER FOUR	36

INTRODUCTION

A marketing director from a large creative agency once told me, 'Always concentrate on producing great work, and never let the client interfere with the creative process. Clients come to you for guidance on each project, so you should be prescriptive about the work you give them. The day you start to care about their input - is the day you should get out of the businesses. Astonishing isn't it, and I completely disagree.

The agency in question, (which will forever remain nameless), had won sack loads of awards for its creativity. No doubt everyone who worked there was very smug and felt extremely pleased with themselves - but what did their client really think about the service they received? Were they happy with it? Was the effectiveness of client campaigns ever measured or followed up on? I wonder.

In my view, all work you complete as a freelance copywriter or creative professional should start from the perspective of respecting your client. You should listen to the individual needs of each client and understand how their company works. Equally, you should attempt to get to know your key contacts as real people - not merely 'consumers' of your creative genius.

If you start each project from this platform of respect, the client will love your work and the respect will be mutual. They will appreciate your personal service and your willingness to understand their company ethos, and you may even come to be viewed as part of their team - which is great for repeat business. .

CHAPTER ONE

What Is a Copywriter and What Does a Copywriter Do?

A copywriter is a person tasked to write the text used for advertisements in magazines, newspapers, television, radio and other kinds of media. A copywriter may also be assigned to come up with the words for press releases, informational or promotional pamphlets, and other promotional materials. A copywriter may also be tasked to rewrite or edit existing materials. Thus, a copywriter's job is a very flexible and potentially exciting career in the wide world of advertising and marketing.

Where Does a Copywriter Work?

A copywriter usually works in advertising firms, retail stores, and marketing companies in a metropolitan area. The working environment of a copywriter is usually found to be ☐uite hectic, which makes creativity under pressure necessary. Advertising is known to be a very fast-paced field where many crises can suddenly occur. A copywriter is usually pressured by short deadline and successive

Assignments daily. A copywriter is often asked for several revisions at the last minute. This job is therefore not for the weak-hearted or the unengaged.

How Fulfilling Is a Copywriter's Job?

Novice and assistant copywriters usually start off with an annual salary of about $30,000 to $35,000 working it up to some $40,000 when they become full-pledged. A senior copywriter may eventually earn some $100,000 a year and about $125,000 if he or she becomes promoted as copywriting chief. A copywriter has the potential to later become creative director and earn as much as $200,000 annually.

A copywriter, like most other workers, is usually required to work 40 hours a week, but it is usually expected to have a lot of overtime in this career. Fortunately overtime is compensated accordingly. A copywriter becomes most busy during key times depending on the nature of their firm's trade - department store copywriters work most during holiday and sale seasons, advertising copywriters work a lot during big advertising campaigns.

Many copywriters today are privileged with profit-sharing schemes afforded by their company. A copywriter also gets the usual benefits such as paid vacations and holidays, pension plans, health care, hospitalization insurance and life insurance. Copywriting can be quite a rewarding job.

How to Become a Copywriter?

A copywriter is expected to be skilled in coming up with great advertising ideas as well as putting them to paper in a very articulate and effective manner. A copywriter should also have a good grasp of layout and typography because visuals are also very important in advertising.

Most advertising agencies require aspiring copywriters to have a solid background in the field, preferably working for at least three years in the business. Copywriters are of course expected to have obtained a college degree, usually in liberal arts, communications, business management, and marketing. A lot of copywriters take college courses that combine creative writing with marketing and this prepares them well for a good copywriting career.

To get hired as a copywriter, one has to be able to combine a solid formal education with an active writing experience. Most copywriters not only had degrees in communications or business, but they actually wrote while studying whether in school publications or community newsletters. A good idea is to present well-written works such as essays and articles.

Are there Opportunities for Growth for a Copywriter?

There is much room for growth for a copywriter. Copywriters working in department stores can become chief of copywriting or fashion coordinator and work their way to become division manager and even advertising chief. Copywriters working in advertising agencies may be promoted as copy supervisor, advancing to copy chief, and then account executive, and ultimately to creative directorship. A copywriter's job can indeed be ⬜uite fulfilling.

In the growing world of business and advertising a copywriter can find a great home with many opportunities for earning and career expansion. Some people undermine the work of copywriters merely because their job seems to be placed at the bottom of the bureaucracy. However a copywriter with the right determination and skill can definitely work his or her way to the top the way their more business-oriented peers do.

Copywriting can be a very fulfilling career for those who have the right skills for the job. If you are full of bright ideas and know how to write well then you might want to try out becoming a copywriter.

Make Your Career As a Copywriter

The copywriter's words are what sell a product or service to the public. A copywriter is responsible for writing the copy for advertisement working in an organization or publishing company. Main duties of a copywriter are developing the ideas and concepts that sell products. The goal is to come up with some new information about the products and services provided by the company.

Copywriter has great scope in variety of fields like writing radio scripts, writing copy for billboards or advertising agency, writing copies for sales letters, direct mails, brochures, posters, booklets, manuals etc.

A copywriter working in a agency needs excellent writing skills, should have good grammar and spelling skills. You can get better experience by practice. There is not specific degree needed to make career in this field. Although there are many universities and colleges that provide some courses related with copywriting like journalism, advertising, communication, English, public relations, mass communication, but anyone can be a copywriter if having good communication and writing skills. Seminars and additional courses in writing and advertisement are helpful to make perfect your writing skills.

There are many positions as a copywriter itself, as junior copywriter, senior copywriter. Junior copywriter writes copy as well as assisting other copywriters with their projects while senior copywriter may write the headline for an ad and then give it to the individual member to make the body content.

There are some tips for one starting his career as a copywriter:

• Write as much as you can, practice will make you perfect.

• Write in your own style, you can take help of any admired or your favorite content writer, but don't copy as it is, write it in your own style.

• Make practice to read magazines and newspapers daily. It will improve your communication skills.

• Get a list of advertising agencies on google, place your cover letter and CV there. Put some thoughts of you on cover letter.

• You can get experience by doing work in advertising agencies, press, newspaper, magazine department.

• Join advertising trade seminars to grow your knowledge.

These tips will help you when starting career as a copywriter.

7 Signs That You Have It in You to Start a Successful Career As a Copywriter!

Your first love is words: If while reading an article, your eyes hooked on to some new word or usage of a word, then you have all the chances of becoming a copywriter. A copywriter's first love is words and he/she is fascinated by new words, find their meaning in dictionary, himself has lot of dictionaries, and use the new words learnt in his/her communication and also knows how to play with words. You understand that these days, less is more, so writing short and crisp copies is the need of the hour.

You have that poetic flair in you: You are mine, until you keep me fine! (LOL) This is not a poem, writing rhyming sentences does not necessarily mean a poem, a poem is a collection of words which are somewhere related to human emotions, so if you write, The last time my heart beat was when I saw you! It □ualifies to be a poem. If you have a knack of writing such poetic content, you □ualify to be a copywriter.

You are well read: If you spent at least 2-3 hours daily in reading and if your WPM (Words Per Minute) is more than 50, then there are fair chances that you will be hired by an agency as copywriter. Actually reading helps you to gain knowledge, knowledge of sectors, industries, economics, companies, latest happenings, politics, films, literature, arts and music, various styles of writing, tone of writing, sentence formation, stories both fiction and non-fiction and a lot more. Years' of investment in reading yields return when you opt to be a copywriter. Reading gives you thought and direction, how to use words and which word should be used at what place.

You are well connected and regularly visit social networking sites: This does not mean that you change your profile pic daily or update your status like "nina@xyz" feeling excited, seriously this does not mean that you are well connected on social media platforms. Being connected here means that you regularly visit sites like Facebook, follow tweets and have followers too, have an updated LinkedIn profile and is actively connected in circles through Google+. When you are active at these platforms, you are exposed to lot of information, happenings, events and other readable stuff and videos. This again gives you plethora of knowledge which you can then apply in your copywriting.

You have the ability to think: This is tough and them you would say, who does not have this ability, we all think. Yes, thinking is one aspect, but the major aspect is how to make use of thoughts and ideas and how to implement them. Can you think of some promotion strategy for an advertising agency? Now most of you might say, print ad, website, radio ad etc. Why can't we think of some out of the box ideas like innovative bookmarks to be given with every book in a bookshop or a CD of Indian Classical or timeless songs given by executives to their clients in the very first meeting. This is where thinking applies and as a copywriter you should be outstanding at it.

You understand that every product or service is a solution which the customer looks forward to: What a business sells is a product, service, idea or concept; however what a customer buys is solution. A customer always look forward to an immediate solution to his problem or need, if my Laptop is crashed, I need to get it fixed as soon as possible, here what I am looking for is a company's technician to immediately respond and fix up my problem. So if you understand this basic need identification and solution e☐uation for almost all sets of business and if you are crystal clear as to who is your target customer, believe me, you are on your way to be an awesome copywriter.

You can spot even a minor grammatical and spelling/punctuation error: This is basic! Seems so. I saw a man-eating tiger in the jungle, or I saw a man eating tiger in the jungle" what is the difference, if you can spot that, you are truly a copywriter ever agency dreams of.

CHAPTER TWO

Your Copywriting Business - What Services Will You Offer?

Whether you're new to setting up a copywriting services business, or are an established copywriter, there are many services you can offer. In this article, we'll look at just seven of them.

Copywriters usually offer two or three of these services, although many just offer one: copywriting.

Let's look at the seven:

1. Copywriting Only - you just write copy

A "copywriting only" copywriter offers just one service: writing. He often has a subcontractor relationship with one or more advertising or graphics' design agencies. Design and marketing decisions on projects are made by someone else.

You can develop a lucrative career as a Copywriting Only copywriter, but you will often face time pressures when several clients simultaneously demand copy. Unfortunately there's no way around these "I need it in 48 hours" demands: you'll be brought in late in a project's evolution (although you'll argue that you should be brought in earlier, this is ignored), so you need to be able to think and write quickly.

2. Marketing pro - you're both a copywriter and marketer

As a marketing copywriter, you're a strategist. You may oversee the complete launch of a new product or service, or you may offer advice in areas like Search Engine Marketing (SEM) with which agency copywriters are unfamiliar.

Marketing copywriters usually have a background in marketing, and although they're paid in line with their experience and skills, they take on fewer projects per year than straight copywriters because the projects are more complex.

3. Public Relations specialist - you're a PR spin doctor

If you enjoy Public Relations copywriting and have contacts at newspapers and magazines, you can become a PR specialist. As a PR copywriter, you're paid for your contacts - your ability to get publicity for your clients.

4. Copy makeover specialist - you critique and rewrite others' copy

Some copywriters add critiquing services to their copywriting services. You revise and revamp copy written by a business's marketing staff. This can be lucrative, but you need diplomacy for this area.

5. Project manager - you handle compete projects, sub-contracting design and marketing

As a project manager, you're a team leader. You organize complete projects, managing the marketing, the design and the copy. You'll sub-contact the work to others, overseeing the entire project, and ensuring that milestones and deadlines are met.

6. Copywriting trainer - you teach copywriting

With professional copywriters in huge demand, and charging high fees, many people want to learn copywriting. Not only do they save on copywriting expenses, but they can get projects completed faster, because they're done in-house.

Teaching copywriting is rewarding. You can offer in-person seminars and classes to corporate and other clients, or online classes.

7. Copywriting consultant - you're a strategist

As a copywriting consultant, you're a strategist. You may develop branding concepts, offer publicity campaigns for businesses or individuals, or develop programs to achieve specific results such as generating leads.

A Super-Successful Copywriting Program Boosts Your Conversation Rates - 3 Secrets Revealed

If you're like me, you've heard time and time again that stories sell. Any copywriting program will tell you they rocket your conversion rate like nobody's business.

However, I don't believe that's actually true. At least not for most of the online sales copy I've read over the years.

After numerous promotions and a thriving career as a copywriter- here's what I want you know about copywriting...

Conversion Rate Secret #1: Write in the context of an "abbreviated" story. Be QUICK about it. Because if you don't, here's what happens: You get long-winded and it ꓯuickly becomes boring to the reader. If readers even begin to lose interest in what you're saying... it's OVER. This is sooooo important - it's one of the very first things to know in copywriting.

Conversion Rate Secret #2: You must use your story in a STRATEGIC manner. Do it right and you can weave many compelling stories throughout your copy. (That's usually what I do!)

In copywriting, you need to learn not to throw in a story just for the sake of "having it there." You must learn to quickly see where the story will have the most IMPACT, and where they can use it as a major selling point - instead of just window decoration.

Conversion Rate Secret #3: You have to ENGAGE your reader. You want them to be right there with you - hanging on every word.

Thinking about stories in terms of "abbreviate"... "be strategic"... and "engage" is a lot different than merely thinking in terms of "offering a solution", "explaining", or "pleading your case", right? So how do your properly abbreviate your story? It's simple, and it's something that heavily stress in my copywriting. All you have to do is take a slice of the story and think about its purpose.

MEET this purpose, and you're done.

If you're good at your craft, I guarantee you can take 3 or 4 lines in a story paragraph -- and with a little effort -- condense it to 1 short, crisp sentence. Keep in mind that if you really engage your prospects, you'll never have to feel shameful or try hiding the fact that you're selling something.

When you do your copy well, your readers will even be eagerly anticipating your offer and wondering what they're going to get!

WEBSITE COPYWRITTING

There are a lot of people today who want to be a copywriter. Besides, this profession is very rewarding and can definitely let you earn a lot of money. This profession is also a great way to help you make extra cash if you already have a regular job.

However, it is also a fact that there are also a lot of people who failed or who aren't really growing in this kind of profession. This is because they tend to forget some of the necessary things in website copywriting.

These necessary things are so minute yet so important in the website copywriting world that many copywriters tend to forget to include these things in their profession.

The very first thing that you have to have in the website copywriting world is a website. Your copywriting website will act as your home base. This will be your office and this is where your clients will hire your services as a copywriter.

Most copywriters do this mistake because they think that being a freelance copywriter doesn't need a website for them to post their services. They usually think that posting in freelance bulletin websites is enough. However, with a website, you will look more professional and more dedicated in your work. If you don't have a website, you will look like a rag-tag freelance copywriter. So, if you don't have a website, you better consider building one or hire someone to build it for you.

Now that you have your website up and running with sample articles and all the links and buttons are fully operational, the next thing you need to do as a freelance website copywriter is to let people in the internet know about it. You have to let people know that your website exists and they should try and visit it.

Since there are a lot of websites like yours in the internet, you have to effectively market your website. So, how will you be able to do this? The best way to do this is through article marketing. Through article marketing, you will increase your market exposure and tell the world about your copywriting skills and at the same time, advertise your services.

All you need to do is write a sample article about a particular subject you are interested in. Don't forget to include a short bio about yourself, and never forget to include a link or URL of your website. This is where people will visit your website.

Post your articles in famous article posting websites. It's free and a lot of people search these websites for practically any subject they want to know about. People search these websites for tips and also for additional knowledge about anything they are interested in. This is why it is important that your article should be keyword rich in order for people to find your articles fast.

As you can see, the two things that you need to do as a website copywriter is very simple and very essential in your career as a copywriter. This is why it is important that you should never forget these two simple yet effective things when you are considering being a website copywriter.

Building your own website and advertising it through article marketing are the two things that you can do to pave your road to success.

CHAPTER THREE

How to Write Like the Top Copywriters

There is a special short-cut to becoming very good at copywriting very quickly. All you need is a great sales letter, a pen and a notebook. The process I'm about to share with you is recommended by all top copywriters in terms of understanding what makes a good sales letter work and developing the habits of legendary copywriters. It's strikingly simple but profoundly effective.

Here's the secret: hand copy top performing sales pages and letters by hand. Yes, it is that simple. It's so simple that many people shrug it off and skip this step while trying to get good. If you hand copy 100 letters by hand you will be well ahead of your peers, believe me.

The first (and most challenging) part of the process is to find a sales letter to copy from. Whatever you do, don't go around the internet looking for a sales page that "looks" good. You could be staring at a visually impressive piece with next to no sales. Only use proven masters.

The people who have written million-dollar sales letters include John Carlton, Gary Halbert, Dan Kennedy, and Harlan Kilstein. If you Google "____ sales letters" and put your copywriter of choice in the blank, you'll find places to download the prized sales letters. Be forewarned that a lot of these will be copyrighted, so make sure you pay for the content if the author has put it on sale. I paid about $150 off Amazon for Harlan Kilstein's collection of sales letters (called "Steal This book") and it was worth every penny. Remember that you are investing in your career as a copywriter or in your ability to write powerful sales copy as a business owner.

Next, get notebook/pad and a pen. It's very important that you copy by hand and not type it up. There's something about actually handwriting that drills the rhythm of the copy into your brain.

Copy the format of the sales page or letter as much as possible. If a word is underlined, then underline it when you re-write the piece. If a line is in bold, I will put "(b)" in front and at the end of the phrase. If a line is in italics, I will put "(i)" in front and at the end of the phrase. Some people I know will just make the ink really heavy for bold, or make their handwriting fancy for italics, but not all of us are that dexterous.

Do this for the entire sales letter, and not just part, so you get the flow of the sales writing into your veins. If you can, finish the whole sales letter in a day. The less you stretch out the hand-copying, the better you'll adopt the patterns of the great copywriters.

This is easy to do, and will really pay off as you increase you copywriting skills. Good luck.

The Ethics of Copywriting - Writing with Respect

A marketing director from a large creative agency once told me, 'Always concentrate on producing great work, and never let the client interfere with the creative process. Clients come to you for guidance on each project, so you should be prescriptive about the work you give them. The day you start to care about their input - is the day you should get out of the businesses. Astonishing isn't it, and I completely disagree.

The agency in □uestion, (which will forever remain nameless), had won sack loads of awards for its creativity. No doubt everyone who worked there was very smug and felt extremely pleased with themselves - but what did their clients really think about the service they received? Were they happy with it? Was the effectiveness of client campaigns ever measured or followed up on? I wonder.

In my view, all work you complete as a freelance copywriter or creative professional should start from the perspective of respecting your clients. You should listen to the individual needs of each client and understand how their company works. Equally, you should attempt to get to know your key contacts as real people - not merely 'consumers' of your creative genius.

If you start each project from this platform of respect, the client will love your work and the respect will be mutual. They will appreciate your personal service and your willingness to understand their company ethos, and you may even come to be viewed as part of their team - which is great for repeat business.

Further to this, when you write copy that respects your clients, and their customers too, this is reflected in the believable tone of your writing. Your target audience is never stupid, and they will always read between the lines of what you're directly saying. So, if you're insincere or take them for granted - this will be reflected in poor sales. If you're respectful and honest, your readers will instantly find you credible and authoritative - and will be more inclined to trust and buy from you.

It's also important to follow up on each project to build on this relationship of mutual respect with the client. Monitor the results of a direct mail campaign or check the response rates from a sales letter you've written. Go back and ask the client how your copy or creative is working out for them - offer to tweak a headline here or a paragraph there to make them happy. You'll be rewarded with great testimonials and more business in future.

Ultimately, respecting both clients and readers will stand you in good stead for your future career as a copywriter or creative professional. It may sound obvious, but it's relatively easy to develop a bit of an ego and start taking things for granted - especially when the money starts rolling in. In the long run, you may not win a sack load of awards for your work, but you will win a sack load of respect and fantastic feedback. You'll also have the satisfaction of knowing you did a good job and genuinely helped your client's business. That always feels great - because at the end of the day, it's not all about the money and industry acclaim. In the end, a truly great copywriter or creative professional is always recognisable by their long list of satisfied clients.

Copywriting in Today's Competitive Market

How to Create More Profitable Creatives

Today's copywriting market is not just competitive, but cutthroat as well. There are beginner copywriters who are willing to work for as little as $2 an ad and work their way up the chain. Then, you have the professional copywriters who can earn thousands of dollars with a single page.

The difference between the two groups is a matter of experience and results. Whereas the beginner is still learning how to use words in the right order and which ones result in more clicks, the professional has a collection of tried and true phrases no matter what business type they are writing for. So how do you stand out in between these two groups and make a profit for your efforts? How do you ensure that your creatives are sought after among the several competitors at your level? There are some very effective tools you can use from the beginning to make sure this happens.

First, you need to pay attention to the ads that get your attention. Why did they get their attention? What specific reason did you continue to read all the way down the page? If the ad is affecting you like that, it will certainly be that way for other consumers. Those that create results should be kept in a folder for your collection. Try to collect ads of different types so you have a wider resource library.

Secondly, there are books to assist copywriters in both general layout and phrasing. Reading those once or more will give you ideas if nothing else. Usually, there are plenty of examples to consider and you'll learn the most current methods being used. Stay updated on your copywriting education so you are always prepared for any challenge.

Third, don't be afraid of a challenge. If you see an ad re☐uest, whether it's for low pay or not, that really seems to stretch your abilities-go for it. Even if you don't submit it, go ahead and write a creative out as if you were. This will give you good practice material to work with, even without the additional pressure of submission.

The more you do these things, the more confident you will start to feel. This immediately helps you tackle bigger opportunities and not worry so much about failure. The fear of failure can often keep you from even considering a major ad request, and this will certainly keep you from growing in your copywriting career.

Finally, create your own voice. Although a company may be looking for a particular tone in their advertising, there is also a reason why they seek you out. You may approach the jobs with a different attitude or sense of personality than other copywriters. This will show itself in your writing, even when you try to hide it.

This voice or personality is a way to make you unique in the copywriting market. When clients start to see results in their ads because of the additional writer's tone, they will return to you for future projects as well.

CHAPTER FOUR

Career Copywriter - 5 Easy Steps to Writing Magnetic Headlines

As a career copywriter it is your goal to create copy that both captivates the reader and drives the bottom line. The most important part of that winning combination is crafting a headline that instills the reader with an irresistible urge to read the rest of the page.

If you really want to be a career copywriter mastering the art of the headline is one of the most important things that you will ever do. 80% of all sales are either won or lost simply through the power of the headline.

Here are 5 time-tested and proven headline writing tips for the career copywriter.

1.) Use headline formulas that work.

These headline formulas would not be in use if they did not work and as a career copywriter you should be taking advantage of them. Here are a few examples

Little Known Ways to *blank*

Here is a Method that is Helping *blank* to *blank*

Who Else Wants *blank*?

The Secret of *blank*

Get Rid of *problem* Once and For All

Here is a Quick Way to *solve a problem*

2.) Use "Quotations" around your Headlines

Quotation marks used around the headline give it the appearance of a testimonial, and as any career copywriter might know the power of peer persuasion can be truly awesome.

3.) Size

Size matters! Many copywriters resort to thinking that bigger is always better but nothing could be farther from the truth. A career copywriter must realize that a headline should stand out but still be readable and kept in comparable scale with the rest of the copy font used in the sales page.

4.) Never End Your Headline with a Period

In school as children we were taught what punctuation marks mean. We were taught that a period means that we have come to the end of a sentence. As adult consumers that same principle is still in our mind. We come to a period and we think that it is the end. As a career copywriter you never want your reader to think that they have come to the end and should move on. Instead of using a single period try using "..." this will give the impression that there is more to learn and direct the reader to the flow.

5.) Funnel the Flow

As a career copywriter you should think of the sales page as a funnel. The object of a funnel is to gather large amounts of something and send it to a designated location. The same is true with sales copy. Think of the headline as the mouth of the funnel. The object is to interest as many readers as you can and begin to direct them to the call to action as the final objective.

If you want to become a successful career copywriter you must master the art of writing a headline and managing the flow of the sales funnel. If you use tried and true headline formulas, make your headline appear as a testimonial by using quotations, keep the size in proportion with the rest of the copy, avoid using a period at the end of the headline and funnel the flow you will succeed an prosper as a career copywriter.

Freelance Copywriting - Start Building Your New Career

Want to make a six figure income from your writing? Copywriting - writing marketing and sales material for businesses - is a wonderful craft to learn. Not only can you make money almost immediately, but you'll also make more money as your skills build.

Let's look at how you can start building your copywriting career in four easy steps.

1. Pay Attention - Who Buys Copy, and How Do They Use It?

Your first step is to discover what COPY actually is. Copy is everywhere, because every business uses it to sell. Copy can be as diverse as a video script, a one-line "tagline" (slogan for a business), a news release, or an advertisement. If its intent is to SELL something, overtly or not, it's copy. I started my copywriting career writing display advertising for a business I was running. Then I wrote press releases, and video scripts. Soon people approached me to write sales material for them, and my copywriting career was launched.

2. Decide What You'd Like to Write

What would you like to write? Perhaps radio advertising intrigues you. Tape some radio ads, and try writing some of your own. Or perhaps you like the idea of writing brochures. Grab all the brochures you can find, and study the text. Yes, the text. Copywriters write text, graphic designers design, so you don't actually need to concern yourself with layouts of brochures, or any other print copy, nor do you work with printers.

3. Write Some Samples

Now you've found examples of copy you'd enjoy writing, write some samples. Write for fictitious businesses, or write for real businesses. Just create some samples to show what you can do.

4. Promote Your New Business - Get Your First Client

Once you've got some samples of your writing skills, it's time to find your first client or two. As a new copywriter, you'll charge considerably less than a pro, so there's no shortage of small businesses willing to give you a try. At this stage, your main concern is to get the jobs done, and get testimonials for your skill from satisfied clients.

4. Build Your Copywriting Career

Over time, as you continue to get clients and complete copywriting jobs, your skills and your fees will increase. You build your career one client at a time, and one completed copywriting job at a time.

Before you know it, you'll be a respected copywriter with a stable of clients. So get started today.

●

www.ingramcontent.com/pod-product-compliance
Lightning Source LLC
Chambersburg PA
CBHW030519220526
45464CB00006B/2873